ENTREPRENEURSHIP

Thinking and Imagination

Savannah Cleggett

Table of Contents

INTRODUCTION

Entrepreneurship is a unique combination of thinking and imagination. It is the ability to see opportunities where others see only obstacles, and to have the courage to turn those opportunities into reality. Entrepreneurs are driven by a passion to create something new, and they have the ability to think outside the box to come up with innovative solutions to problems. They have the imagination to envision a better future, and the determination to make it happen. Entrepreneurs are the driving force behind the growth and development of the economy, and their contributions are essential for the prosperity of society

Entrepreneurship is a journey of creativity, vision and risk-taking. It requires individuals to think differently, to use their imagination and tap into their inner resources to turn their ideas into successful bus61iness ventures.

Entrepreneurs are not afraid to challenge the status quo and think beyond the boundaries of what is considered "normal." They are individuals who are driven by a sense of purpose, who have the courage to pursue their dreams, and the resilience to overcome obstacles. Entrepreneurship is a challenging yet rewarding path, one that allows individuals to create something truly meaningful and make a positive impact on the world. It is the ability to turn one's imagination into a reality and make a difference in society.

Entrepreneurial thinking and margination also require a willingness to take risks. Entrepreneurs need to be willing to put their ideas and plans into action, even if there is a chance of failure. They understand that failure is a natural part of the process and that there is always something to be learned from it.

An entrepreneur who can balance both thinking and imagination is able to make informed decisions, while also being open to new ideas and opportunities. This combination of skills sets them apart and allows them to stand out in a competitive market.

Chapter One

The importance of creative thinking in entrepreneurship

Creative thinking is important in entrepreneurship because it allows entrepreneurs to come up with new and innovative ideas for products, services, and business models. This can give them a competitive advantage and help them stand out in the market. Additionally, creative thinking can also help entrepreneurs find new and unique solutions to problems they encounter in their business, and help them think outside the box when it comes to marketing and other business strategies. In short, creative thinking can be a key driver of success in entrepreneurship, helping entrepreneurs to think differently and achieve more.

Creative thinking is an essential component of entrepreneurship as it allows entrepreneurs to develop new and innovative ideas that can be turned into successful business ventures. It involves using imagination and creativity to generate unique solutions to problems and identify opportunities for growth and development. creative thinking also allows entrepreneurs to identify new opportunities for growth and expansion. For example, an entrepreneur may use creative thinking to identify a new market or target audience for their product or service, leading to increased revenue and success for the business.

How to develop and hone your creative thinking skills

Developing and honing your creative thinking skills is an ongoing process that requires effort and commitment. Here are some ways to do so

1. Practice brainstorming

One of the best ways to develop creative thinking skills is to practice brainstorming. This is the process of generating a large number of ideas without judging or evaluating them. The goal is to generate as many ideas as possible, even if they seem impractical or unrealistic. Learn from others: Surround yourself with people who think creatively and learn from them. This can be done by networking, joining a creative group or association, or reading books and articles about creative thinking.

2. Take on new challenges

Challenge yourself to take on new and unfamiliar tasks that require creative thinking. This can be anything from trying a new hobby or learning a new skill.Entrepreneurship is a mindset and approach to business that involves taking on new challenges and using creativity, imagination, and critical thinking to develop new ideas and opportunities. Entrepreneurs are typically characterized by their willingness to take risks and their ability to think outside of the box. They are also often driven by a passion for their work and a desire to make a positive impact in the world.

3. Get away from the routine

Step out of your comfort zone and expose yourself to new experiences and perspectives. This can be done by traveling, meeting new people, or taking on new projects and start thinking outside the box. Don't be afraid to take risks and try new things. Always be open to new ideas and be willing to adapt to change. Cultivate a strong sense of creativity and imagination, and use it to come up with innovative solutions to problems. And above all, never stop learning and growing. Remember that the road to success is never a straight line, and that there will be bumps and obstacles along the way. But with a strong sense of determination and a willingness to learn from your mistakes, you can achieve your goals and build a successful business.

4. Embrace failure

Failure is a natural part of the creative process. Embrace it and learn from your mistakes. Don't be afraid to experiment and try new things, even if they don't work out.

Embracing failure is the mindset of accepting that failure is a natural part of the entrepreneurial journey. It is understanding that failure is not a setback but rather an opportunity to learn and grow. Entrepreneurs who embrace failure are not afraid to take risks and try new things, even if they may not succeed. They understand that failure is a valuable learning experience that can provide valuable insights and opportunities for growth.

Thinking and imagination play a key role in embracing failure. Entrepreneurs who are able to think creatively and imagine new possibilities are more likely to take risks and try new things. They are able to see beyond the current situation and envision new opportunities for success. Additionally, entrepreneurs who are able to think strategically and plan for potential failure are better equipped to handle the challenges that come with taking risks.

5. Stay curious

Cultivate a curious mindset and keep an open mind. Ask questions, seek out new information and be willing to explore new ideas.

Stay curious" is a phrase that encourages individuals to continue to explore new ideas and perspectives. It highlights the importance of having an open mind and being willing to learn and discover new things.

Being curious as an entrepreneur means being willing to take risks and explore new opportunities. It means being open to new ideas and not being afraid to try something new. It also means being willing to question the status quo and challenge assumptions.

Imagination is also a key component of being an entrepreneur. It allows individuals to think outside of the box and come up with new and innovative solutions to problems. Entrepreneurs who possess a strong imagination are able to visualize new possibilities and create products and services that meet the needs of their customers.

6. Meditate

Meditation can help you focus your mind and reduce stress, which can open up new.
Meditation is a practice that involves focusing the mind on a specific object, thought, or activity to achieve a mentally clear and emotionally calm state. It is often used as a tool for self-reflection and self-improvement, and has been shown to have numerous benefits for both mental and physical health.

In the context of entrepreneurship, meditation can be particularly beneficial for developing thinking and imagination. By regularly taking time to clear the mind and focus on the present moment, entrepreneurs can improve their ability to think creatively and come up with new ideas. Additionally, meditation can help entrepreneurs to better focus and prioritize their thoughts, which can be particularly beneficial when trying to navigate the fast-paced and constantly changing landscape of the business world.

Furthermore, meditation can help entrepreneurs to better manage stress and anxiety, which can often be major obstacles to creativity and productivity. By learning to calm the mind and focus on the present moment, entrepreneurs can reduce the negative effects of stress and anxiety, and be better able to think and imagine new possibilities.

Overall, meditation is a powerful tool that entrepreneurs can use to develop their thinking and imagination, and to improve their overall well-being. By taking time to meditate on a regular basis, entrepreneurs can improve their ability to think creatively, manage stress, and be more productive in their work.

Case studies of successful entrepreneurs who used creative thinking to solve problems and seize opportunities

1. Steve Jobs

Steve Jobs, the co-founder of Apple, was known for his ability to think creatively and come up with innovative solutions. He was able to identify a gap in the market for personal computers and create a new category of products with the launch of the Macintosh computer in 1984. He also revolutionized the music industry with the launch of the iPod and iTunes in 2001. Steve Jobs' creative thinking allowed him to identify new opportunities and solve problems in the tech industry, leading to the success of Apple as a company.

Steven Jobs, the co-founder of Apple, was a master of creative thinking when it came to solving problems and seizing opportunities. One of his most notable examples of this was with the development of the Macintosh computer. In the early 1980s, personal computers were primarily used by businesses and were not yet mainstream in households. Jobs saw an opportunity to create a personal computer that was easy for everyday people to use and understand.

To achieve this, Jobs and his team used creative thinking to design a user-friendly interface that was intuitive and simple to navigate. They also made the computer small and portable, which was a first for personal computers at the time. This allowed people to use the computer in their homes and on the go.

Additionally, they created an advertising campaign that spoke to the everyday person and made them feel like they needed a Macintosh in their lives.

Jobs' creative thinking also helped him solve problems that arose during the development of the Macintosh. For example, when the Macintosh team was struggling to create a font that was both elegant and easy to read, Jobs came up with the solution of hiring a calligrapher to design the font. This led to the creation of the famous "Chicago" font that is still used in Apple products today.

Another example of Jobs' creative problem-solving was when he was developing the iPhone. The initial design for the iPhone included a physical keyboard, but Jobs realized that this would not be as user-friendly as a touch screen interface. He made the bold decision to scrap the physical keyboard and instead focus on developing a touch screen interface. This decision was met with skepticism by many, but Jobs' creative thinking ultimately led to the success of the iPhone.

2. Richard Branson

Richard Branson, the founder of Virgin Group, is another successful entrepreneur who used creative thinking to solve problems and seize opportunities. He started his business by identifying a gap in the market for low-cost, high-quality music and created Virgin Records. He then expanded his business empire to include airlines, hotels, and other industries, all through his ability to think creatively and identify new opportunities.

Richard Branson, the founder of the Virgin Group, is known for his creative thinking and ability to spot opportunities in unexpected places. He started his first business, a student magazine called Student, at the age of 16 and has since gone on to build a diverse portfolio of companies that includes everything from airlines to music labels to health clubs.

One of Branson's most successful ventures was the creation of Virgin Atlantic Airways. In the 1980s, the airline industry was dominated by a few large players, and Branson saw an opportunity to disrupt the market with a new, low-cost airline. He used creative thinking to come up with a new business model that focused on providing high-quality service at a lower cost, and he used his personal brand to generate buzz and attract customers. Virgin Atlantic quickly became a major player in the airline industry, and it continues to be a leader in customer service and innovation today.

Another example of Branson's creative thinking is his decision to launch Virgin Galactic, a space tourism company. While many people thought the idea was crazy, Branson saw an opportunity to bring space travel to the masses and make it accessible to a wider audience. He has invested heavily in research and development, and the company is now on the cusp of launching its first commercial flights.

Overall, Richard Branson's success can be attributed to his ability to think creatively and spot opportunities in unexpected places. He is not afraid to take risks and is always looking for ways to push the boundaries and do things differently. His entrepreneurial spirit and innovative approach have made him one of the most successful and well-known entrepreneurs of our time.

3. Mark Zuckerberg

Mark Zuckerberg, the co-founder and CEO of Facebook, is another example of an entrepreneur who used creative thinking to solve problems and seize opportunities. He identified a gap in the market for a social networking platform and created Facebook in

2004. He then continued to expand and improve the platform, solving problems such as privacy concerns and monetization, through his ability to think creatively.

Mark Zuckerberg is the founder and CEO of Facebook, one of the most successful and influential technology companies in the world. He is a prime example of an entrepreneur who used creative thinking to solve problems and seize opportunities.

In 2004, while studying at Harvard University, Zuckerberg had the idea to create a social networking platform that would connect students on campus. He recognized the need for a more efficient way for students to connect and share information, and used his creative thinking to develop a solution. He created a website called "Thefacebook," which quickly gained popularity among students at Harvard and eventually spread to other universities.

As the website continued to grow, Zuckerberg faced many challenges, including legal disputes over the ownership of the company. However, he was able to navigate these challenges and continue to grow the company by using creative thinking to find solutions.

In 2012, Facebook went public, making Zuckerberg one of the youngest billionaires in the world. Today, Facebook has over 2 billion monthly active users and is a major player in the technology and advertising industries. Zuckerberg's success is a testament to his ability to think creatively and solve problems. He recognized a need in the market and used his skills and resources to create a solution that changed the way we connect and share information online.

4. Elon Musk

Elon Musk, the CEO of SpaceX and Tesla, is another entrepreneur who used creative thinking to solve problems and seize opportunities. He identified a gap in the space industry and created SpaceX to make space travel more affordable and accessible. He also identified a gap in the automotive industry and created Tesla to produce electric cars that are more affordable and efficient. Through his ability to think creatively, he has been able to solve problems and create new opportunities in the space and automotive industries.

Elon Musk is a successful entrepreneur known for his innovative and creative thinking. He is the CEO of SpaceX, Tesla, Neuralink, and The Boring Company.

One example of Musk using creative thinking to solve a problem is with SpaceX. When SpaceX first started, the cost of launching a rocket into space was extremely high and the success rate was low. Musk had the creative idea to develop reusable rockets, which would significantly reduce the cost of space launches.

After many failed attempts, SpaceX finally succeeded in landing the first stage of its Falcon 9 rocket back on Earth in 2015. This breakthrough has since been a game-changer in the aerospace industry, making space launches more affordable and reliable.

Another example of Musk using creative thinking to seize opportunities is with Tesla. When Musk first started Tesla, electric cars were seen as a niche market with limited potential. However, Musk had a vision of creating a mass-market for electric cars and he used creative thinking to make this a reality.

He has been able to make electric cars more affordable, improve their range and charging infrastructure, and make them more desirable to consumers. This has led to a significant increase in the number of electric cars on the road, and has helped to pave the way for a more sustainable future.

5. Oprah Winfrey

Oprah Winfrey, the media mogul, is another successful entrepreneur who used creative thinking to solve problems and seize opportunities. She identified a gap in the talk show industry and created her own show, "The Oprah Winfrey Show. "She then expanded her brand to include her own magazine, a production company, and a book club. Through her ability to think creatively, she has been able to solve problems and create new opportunities in the media industry, leading to her success as an entrepreneur.

Oprah Winfrey is one of the most successful and influential entrepreneurs of our time. She is best known for her talk show, "The Oprah Winfrey Show," which ran for 25 years and made her one of the most powerful and influential women in the world.

Oprah's success story began in the 1970s, when she was working as a news anchor in Nashville, Tennessee. She was frustrated with the lack of opportunities for African-American women in the media, and decided to take matters into her own hands.

In 1976, she moved to Baltimore and landed a job as the host of a local talk show called "People Are Talking." The show was a huge success, and soon Oprah was offered her own nationally syndicated talk show, "The Oprah Winfrey Show."

The show was an instant hit, and Oprah quickly became one of the most influential figures in the entertainment industry. She used her platform to address important social issues, and to give a voice to marginalized communities.

Oprah's creative thinking and ability to solve problems helped her to seize opportunities and build a media empire. She used her platform to create a number of successful spin-off shows, such as "Dr. Phil" and "Rachael Ray."

In addition to her television empire, Oprah has also built a successful career as an actress, author, and philanthropist. She has used her wealth and influence to support a number of charitable causes, and has been a powerful advocate for education and women's rights.

Oprah's story is a testament to the power of creative thinking and the ability to solve problems. She has used her talents and resources to create a successful career and make a positive impact on the world.

Chapter Two

The power of visualization and visualization techniques

Visualization, also known as mental imagery or mental rehearsal, is the process of creating mental images of a desired outcome or goal. This technique can be used in various areas of life, including business, sports, and personal development. For entrepreneurs, visualization can be a powerful tool for achieving success. By visualizing their goals and the steps needed to achieve them, entrepreneurs can clarify their vision and increase their motivation to work towards their objectives. By visualizing themselves successfully completing a task or achieving a specific goal, entrepreneurs can build confidence in their abilities and increase their chances of success. Visualization techniques vary, but some common methods include:

1. Mind mapping

This technique involves creating a visual representation of your ideas and goals by connecting them in a diagram-like format. It helps to organize your thoughts and see connections between different ideas.

Visualization is the practice of creating mental images or pictures in one's mind in order to achieve a specific goal or outcome. It is a powerful tool that can be used to improve focus, concentration, motivation, and overall well-being.

One popular visualization technique is mind mapping. Mind mapping is a visual representation of ideas, concepts, and information in the form of a diagram or map. It is a way of organizing and connecting information in a visual and logical way.

To create a mind map, start with a central idea or topic and branch out to related ideas, concepts, and information. Use different colors, shapes, and images to represent different types of information. This can help to make the information more memorable and easier to understand.

Mind mapping can be used for a variety of purposes, such as brainstorming, problem-solving, and planning. It is a great tool for students, as it can help them to organize and understand complex information. It can also be used for project management, as it can help to identify and organize tasks and deadlines.

2. Affirmations

Affirmations are positive statements that you repeat to yourself, either out loud or in your mind. They can help to visualize your goals and reinforce the belief that you can achieve them. Visualization is a powerful tool that can help individuals achieve their goals and improve their overall well-being. It involves creating mental images of a desired outcome or situation, and focusing on those images to manifest them in reality. Visualization techniques can be used in a variety of ways, including for personal development, health and wellness, and career advancement.

Affirmations are a common visualization technique that can be used to improve self-esteem and confidence, overcome limiting beliefs, and achieve specific goals. Affirmations are positive statements that are repeated regularly to oneself, with the intention of making them a reality. For example, an affirmation might be "I am confident and successful in my career" or "I am healthy and fit." By repeating these statements regularly, individuals can begin to believe them and take actions that align with them.

Visualization and affirmation techniques are particularly effective when used in combination. By visualizing a desired outcome and repeating positive affirmations related to that outcome, individuals can create a powerful mental image that can motivate them to take action and achieve their goals. Additionally, visualization and affirmation techniques can be used to overcome negative thoughts and beliefs, and to build a positive mindset.

3. Role-playing

This technique involves imagining yourself in a scenario where your goal has already been achieved. This can help to create a sense of excitement and motivation to work towards your goal.

Visualization is the practice of using your imagination to create mental images of something you want to achieve or accomplish. It is a powerful tool that can help you to manifest your goals and desires by bringing them to life in your mind.

Role-playing is a visualization technique that involves acting out a scenario in your mind as if it were happening in real life. This can be a powerful way to visualize your goals and desires, as it allows you to experience them in a realistic and tangible way.

For example, if you want to become a successful entrepreneur, you can use role-playing to visualize yourself running your own business, making deals, and achieving success. By acting out this scenario in your mind, you can start to feel the emotions and energy associated with achieving your goal, which can help to motivate and inspire you to take action.

Role-playing can also be used to overcome fears and obstacles. For example, if you are afraid of public speaking, you can use role-playing to visualize yourself giving a successful speech, and experiencing the positive emotions and confidence that come with it.

Overall, visualization and visualization techniques like role-playing can be powerful tools for achieving your goals and desires. They can help you to bring your goals to life in your mind, and to overcome any obstacles or fears that may be holding you back.

4. Imaginary walk-through

This technique involves visualizing yourself walking through the steps required to achieve your goal. It can help to identify any potential obstacles or challenges that need to be overcome.

Visualization is the process of creating mental images or pictures of something that is not physically present. It can be used to visualize goals, dreams, or ideas in order to make them more concrete and attainable. Visualization techniques can be used to help people achieve their goals, overcome fears, and improve their mental and physical health.

One visualization technique that is commonly used is the imaginary walk-through. This technique involves creating a mental image of a specific environment or situation, and then "walking" through it in your mind. This can be used to visualize a future goal, such as a new job or home, or to practice for an upcoming event, such as a public speaking engagement.

To use the imaginary walk-through technique, start by finding a quiet and comfortable place to sit or lie down. Close your eyes and take a few deep breaths to relax your body and mind. Next, create a mental image of the environment or situation you want to visualize. Imagine yourself walking through the space, noticing all of the details and sensory information. Pay attention to the sights, sounds, smells, and feelings that you experience as you move through the space.

As you walk through your imagined environment, you can also practice different behaviors or actions. For example, if you are visualizing a job interview, imagine yourself answering questions confidently and calmly. If you are visualizing a home, imagine yourself cooking a meal in the kitchen or relaxing in the living room.

By regularly practicing the imaginary walk-through technique, you can make your goals and dreams more concrete and attainable, and increase your confidence and preparedness for real-life situations.

5. Goal board

This technique involves creating a visual representation of your goals by creating a board or a poster with pictures and words related to your goals. It can serve as a daily reminder of your goals and progress.

Visualization is the act of creating a mental image or scenario in your mind. It is a powerful tool that can be used to achieve goals, overcome obstacles, and improve overall well-being. Visualization techniques involve using specific methods to create and maintain a clear image or scenario in your mind.

One popular visualization technique is creating a goal board. A goal board is a visual representation of your goals and aspirations, typically created on a poster board or bulletin board. It can include pictures, quotes, and other visual elements that represent your goals and the steps you need to take to achieve them. Goal boards serve as a constant reminder of your goals and help to keep you motivated and focused on achieving them. They can also help to break down larger goals into smaller, more manageable steps, making them more attainable.

Creating a goal board is simple and can be done with materials you have around the house. Start by identifying your goals, both short-term and long-term. Then, gather pictures, quotes, and other visual elements that represent those goals and place them on your goal board. Place the goal board in a place where you will see it often, such as your bedroom or office.

How to use visualization to turn your ideas into reality

Visualization is a powerful tool for entrepreneurs to turn their ideas into reality. It is a technique where one imagines a desired outcome or goal in their mind, as if it has already happened. By visualizing the end result, entrepreneurs can create a clear mental picture of what they want to achieve and take the necessary steps to make it happen.

One way to use visualization is to create a Vision board. A vision board is a collage of images and words that represent your goals and aspirations. It can be a physical board or a digital one. The key is to choose images and words that align with your goals and that resonate with you emotionally. By looking at your vision board daily, you will be reminded of your goals and it will help to keep you motivated.

Another way to use visualization is to Practice Mindfulness. Mindfulness is the practice of being present in the moment and focusing on your thoughts and feelings. By being present and aware of your thoughts, you can identify any negative thoughts or limiting beliefs that may be holding you back. Once you identify these thoughts, you can replace them with positive and empowering thoughts. This will help you to stay focused and motivated on your goals.

Lastly, visualization can be used to plan and organize your goals. By visualizing the steps needed to achieve your goals, you can create a plan of action. You can also use visualization to break down your goals into smaller, manageable tasks. This will make it easier for you to stay on track and achieve your goals.

Example of successful entrepreneurs who used visualization to achieve their goals

Visualization, or the act of creating mental images of desired outcomes, is a powerful tool that successful entrepreneurs use to achieve their goals. By visualizing their desired outcome, entrepreneurs are able to focus their thoughts and energy on the end result, which in turn, helps them to take the necessary steps to make it a reality.

One example of a successful entrepreneur who used visualization to achieve their goals is Oprah Winfrey. Oprah has stated that she always visualized herself as a successful talk show host, and even went as far as creating a vision board with pictures of herself on a talk show set. This visualization helped her to focus her energy and efforts on becoming a successful talk show host, which ultimately led to her becoming one of the most successful and influential entrepreneurs in the media industry.

Another example is Tony Robbins, a motivational speaker, and author who is known for his use of visualization techniques in his coaching and personal development programs. Robbins encourages his clients to visualize their desired outcomes, and then take the necessary steps to make them a reality.

Through visualization, Robbins has helped thousands of entrepreneurs and individuals to achieve their goals and live their best lives.

Steve Jobs, the founder of Apple, is also known to have used visualization to achieve his goals. Jobs had a clear vision of what he wanted to achieve with Apple and he used visualization to help him stay focused on that vision. He would constantly visualize the end result and work towards it. This helped him to develop some of the most iconic products in the history of technology, such as the iPhone, iPad, and Mac.

Chapter Three

The role of risk-taking in entrepreneurship

Risk-taking is an essential component of entrepreneurship. Starting and growing a business often involves taking on significant financial, operational, and personal risks. Entrepreneurs must be willing to invest time, money, and energy into their ideas, even when there is no guarantee of success. They must also be willing to make bold decisions and take calculated risks to move their business forward. Without a willingness to take risks, entrepreneurs may miss out on opportunities to innovate, grow, and succeed in their field. Additionally, taking risks can help entrepreneurs build resilience and adapt to changing market conditions. Overall, risk-taking is a key attribute of successful entrepreneurs, and it is necessary for them to reach their goals.

Entrepreneurship is all about taking risks. Without the willingness to take risks, an entrepreneur would not be able to start a new business or venture. Risk-taking is an essential part of the entrepreneurial process, as it allows entrepreneurs to think outside of the box and imagine new possibilities.

Thinking and imagination are key components of risk-taking in entrepreneurship. Entrepreneurs must be able to think creatively and imagine new ideas and opportunities. They must be able to see potential where others see only obstacles. This ability to think and imagine is what allows entrepreneurs to identify and seize new opportunities, even in the face of uncertainty and risk.

Risk-taking also requires a strong sense of self-confidence. Entrepreneurs must believe in themselves and their ideas, even when others are skeptical. They must be willing to put their own money, time, and reputation on the line to pursue their dreams. This takes a great deal of courage and determination, which are also important traits for successful entrepreneurs.

Understanding and managing risk in the entrepreneurial

Entrepreneurship is all about taking risks. Without the ability to think creatively and imagine new possibilities, entrepreneurs would never be able to identify and pursue new opportunities. However, it is important to understand that not all risks are created equal. Some risks may be much more significant than others, and it is essential for entrepreneurs to be able to identify and manage these risks in order to be successful.

Understanding Risk will help to identifying the potential risks that are associated with a particular venture, and then evaluating the likelihood and impact of each risk. For example, a new product launch may be risky because it is untested in the market. However, if the entrepreneur has conducted extensive market research and has a solid marketing plan, the risk may be considered manageable.

Develop a Strategy For Managing Them. This may involve implementing risk management techniques such as diversifying investments, creating contingency plans, and insuring against potential losses. It may also involve forming partnerships and collaborations with other businesses or individuals who can help mitigate the risks.

Imagination is also a crucial component of managing risk in the entrepreneurial process. Entrepreneurs who are able to think creatively and come up with new solutions to problems are better able to identify and manage risks. For example, an entrepreneur who can imagine new ways to reach customers or new ways to manufacture a product may be able to reduce the risks associated with a new venture.

Case studies of entrepreneurs who took calculated risks and reaped the rewards

Entrepreneurship is all about thinking and imagination. It requires individuals to think outside the box, to come up with innovative ideas, and to take calculated risks in order to achieve success. The following are case studies of entrepreneurs who took calculated risks and heaped the rewards

1. Jeff Bezos, Founder and CEO of Amazon

Jeff Bezos is one of the most successful entrepreneurs of our time. He founded Amazon in 1994, when online retail was still in its infancy. Despite the risk of investing in an untested market, Bezos had the foresight to see the potential of e-commerce and took the risk to launch Amazon. Today, Amazon is one of the largest and most successful companies in the world, and Bezos is one of the wealthiest individuals on the planet.

2. Mark Zuckerberg, Founder and CEO of Facebook

Mark Zuckerberg founded Facebook in 2004 while he was still a student at Harvard University. Despite the skepticism of many, Zuckerberg took the risk to launch Facebook, which quickly became one of the most popular social networking sites in the world. Today, Facebook is one of the most valuable companies in the world, and Zuckerberg is one of the wealthiest individuals on the planet.

3. Elon Musk, Founder and CEO of SpaceX and Tesla

Elon Musk is a visionary entrepreneur who has taken on some of the biggest risks in the business world. He founded SpaceX in 2002, with the goal of making space travel affordable and accessible to the masses. Despite the skepticism of many, Musk took the risk to launch SpaceX, which has since become one of the most successful private space companies in the world. Musk also founded Tesla in 2003, with the goal of revolutionizing the auto industry with electric cars. Despite the skepticism of many, Musk took the risk to launch Tesla, which has since become one of the most successful and valuable car companies in the world.

Chapter Four

The importance of resilience and perseverance in entrepreneurship

Resilience and perseverance are essential traits for entrepreneurs. Starting and growing a business can be a challenging and difficult journey, and it is important for entrepreneurs to be able to handle and recover from setbacks.

Resilience allows entrepreneurs to bounce back from failure and keep going, while perseverance helps them to stay focused and motivated in the face of obstacles. Without these traits, it can be easy for entrepreneurs to give up when faced with challenges, and their businesses may not succeed. Additionally, having a strong imagination can help entrepreneurs to come up with new and innovative ideas, which can be critical for success in a competitive market.

Entrepreneurship requires a unique combination of thinking and imagination to be successful. Without the ability to think strategically and creatively, entrepreneurs may struggle to come up with innovative ideas and solutions to problems that arise in the course of building and growing a business.

However, even the best ideas and strategies can fall short without the determination and resilience to see them through. Entrepreneurship is not for the faint of heart, and it can be filled with obstacles and setbacks that can test even the most resilient individual. Resilience is the ability to bounce back from adversity and keep moving forward, even in the face of failure or setback. In entrepreneurship, resilience is essential for overcoming the many obstacles that arise when starting and growing a business. Entrepreneurs need to be able to adapt to changing market conditions and customer needs, as well as navigate the many challenges that come with growing and scaling a business.

Perseverance is also key to success in entrepreneurship. Entrepreneurs need to be able to stay the course and continue to push forward, even when things get tough. This requires a strong sense of commitment and a willingness to work through the challenges that arise along the way.

Coping with setbacks and failures as an entrepreneur

As an entrepreneur, setbacks and failures are an inevitable part of the journey. However, it's important to remember that they are not necessarily a reflection of your abilities or the potential success of your business. Instead, they are opportunities to learn and grow, and to develop the resilience and determination needed to succeed as an entrepreneur.

One key strategy for coping with setbacks and failures is to maintain a positive attitude and to focus on the lessons that can be learned from each experience. This might involve taking time to reflect on what went wrong and what could be done differently in the future, as well as seeking feedback and support from others.

Another important strategy is to set realistic goals and to focus on small, incremental steps towards achieving them. This can help to keep you motivated and focused, even in the face of setbacks and failures. Additionally, it's important to take care of yourself and to find ways to manage stress and maintain balance in your life, as this can help to keep you feeling energized and motivated as you work towards your goals.

Ultimately, the key to coping with setbacks and failures as an entrepreneur is to stay resilient, stay focused on your goals, and to keep learning and growing as you work towards success. With the right mindset and approach, you can overcome any obstacles and achieve your entrepreneurial dreams.

Examples of entrepreneurs who demonstrated resilience and perseverance in the face of adversity

Entrepreneurship is a challenging and often unpredictable journey that requires a combination of both thinking and imagination. It takes a certain type of person to be able to navigate the ups and downs of starting and growing a business. Resilience and perseverance are two key traits that successful entrepreneurs possess and demonstrate in the face of adversity.

One example of an entrepreneur who demonstrated resilience and perseverance is

- **Oprah Winfrey**

Oprah faced many obstacles throughout her career, including poverty, racism, and sexual abuse. Despite these challenges, she was able to overcome them and become one of the most successful and influential figures in media. Oprah's resilience and perseverance were key to her success, as she was able to bounce back from setbacks and keep pushing forward towards her goals.

Oprah Winfrey is a prime example of an entrepreneur who demonstrated resilience and perseverance in the face of adversity. Born into poverty and facing numerous challenges throughout her childhood, including sexual abuse and discrimination, Oprah never let her difficult upbringing hold her back.

Despite these challenges, Oprah was determined to succeed and worked hard to achieve her goals. She excelled academically and was awarded a full scholarship to Tennessee State University, where she studied communication.

After graduation, Oprah began her career in media as a news anchor and eventually transitioned to hosting her own talk show, "The Oprah Winfrey Show," which became one of the most successful and influential talk shows in history.

Throughout her career, Oprah faced numerous obstacles, including criticism and skepticism about her ability to succeed in the male-dominated world of television. However, she persevered and continued to push herself, eventually becoming one of the most successful and influential figures in media.

In addition to her successful career, Oprah has also been a philanthropist and has used her resources to help others and make a positive impact on the world. Her resilience and perseverance have not only helped her achieve success but also helped her to make a difference in the lives of others.

- **Mark Zuckerberg**

The founder of Facebook Mark faced many challenges in the early days of the company, including legal battles, privacy concerns, and intense competition from other social media platforms. Despite these challenges, Mark was able to persevere and continue to build Facebook into the global powerhouse it is today. His resilience and perseverance were key to his success, as he was able to navigate the obstacles and continue to innovate and grow the company.

Mark Zuckerberg is the founder and CEO of Facebook, one of the most successful and popular social media platforms in the world. He demonstrated resilience and perseverance in the face of adversity by overcoming a number of challenges throughout the development and growth of his company.

One of the biggest challenges Zuckerberg faced was the legal battle over the ownership of Facebook. In 2004, three former classmates of Zuckerberg's at Harvard, Cameron and Tyler Winklevoss and Divya Narendra, claimed that Zuckerberg had stolen their idea for a social networking site called "The Harvard Connection." The legal dispute lasted for several years and even reached the Supreme Court, but Zuckerberg ultimately emerged victorious, with the court ruling in his favor.

Zuckerberg also faced criticism and controversy over issues such as data privacy, the role of fake news on the platform, and the Cambridge Analytica scandal. Despite these challenges, he has persevered and continued to lead Facebook to new heights of success.

In addition, Zuckerberg has also demonstrated resilience and perseverance in his personal life. He and his wife, Priscilla Chan, have been committed to philanthropy and charitable efforts, including the Chan Zuckerberg Initiative, which focuses on education and health initiatives.

- **J.K. Rowling**

The author of the Harry Potter series, is another example of an entrepreneur who demonstrated resilience and perseverance. J.K. Rowling faced rejection from several publishers before finally finding success with her Harry Potter books. Despite the initial rejections, J.K. Rowling never gave up and continued to work on her manuscript. Her resilience and perseverance were key to her success, as she was able to overcome the setbacks and become one of the most successful authors of all time.

J.K. Rowling is a prime example of an entrepreneur who demonstrated resilience and perseverance in the face of adversity. Before becoming a successful author and one of the wealthiest women in the world, Rowling struggled with poverty and personal tragedy.

In the mid-1990s, Rowling was a single mother living on welfare in Edinburgh, Scotland. She had just divorced her husband and was struggling to make ends meet. Despite this, she continued to work on her manuscript for a fantasy novel about a boy wizard named Harry Potter.

After several rejections from publishers, Rowling finally found a small independent publisher who agreed to publish the first Harry Potter book, Harry Potter and the Philosopher's Stone. However, even after the book was published, it faced challenges. Critics initially gave it mixed reviews and it was not an immediate bestseller.

Despite these setbacks, Rowling persevered. She continued to write more Harry Potter books, and with each new release, the series gained more popularity and critical acclaim. Today, the Harry Potter series is one of the best-selling book series of all time, and has been adapted into a successful film franchise.

Through her resilience and perseverance, Rowling was able to turn her passion for writing into a successful career, despite the many challenges she faced along the way. She serves as an inspiration to other entrepreneurs who are facing adversity in their own businesses.

CONCLUSION

In conclusion, the key elements for success as an entrepreneur are thinking and imagination. These two components are essential for coming up with innovative ideas, identifying opportunities, and developing strategies to turn those ideas into reality. A successful entrepreneur must have the ability to think critically and creatively, and to visualize potential outcomes and opportunities. They must also have the imagination to see beyond the current limitations and to envision a better future. With the right combination of thinking and imagination, entrepreneurs can create something new, unique and valuable that can change the world for the better.